PORTFOLIO 4

METROPOLITAN SEMINARS IN ART

Portfolio 4 · *Abstraction*

by John Canaday

ART EDITOR AND CRITIC
THE NEW YORK TIMES

THE METROPOLITAN MUSEUM OF ART

ABSTRACTION

The Painter and the World We Never See

FROM time to time in our discussions we have reminded the reader that the first importance of a painting is not the accuracy with which it reproduces the look of the subject being painted. We have seen some pictures that are known and loved for their subject—"Whistler's Mother" (Plate 1, Portfolio 1) is one of them. But we tried to show that actually the appeal of that picture may come as much from abstract elements as from the subject itself, even when the observer has no idea what these abstract elements are. In the case of "Whistler's Mother" the abstract element is particularly the arrangement (composition) of the various objects in the picture area as shapes that are interesting or expressive just as shapes, without regard to their being also a curtain, a picture on a wall, a lace cap, an old lady's profile, a chair, a floor, or a pair of hands at rest. We said that Whistler himself was insisting on the abstract elements of composition and color when he called the picture *Arrangement in Gray and Black*. It is only the popular appeal of the subject that has so persistently made the picture known by its familiar title of "Whistler's Mother."

Abstract elements were also stressed in our analysis of Renoir's portrait of his wife (Plate 3, Portfolio 1). There we saw natural forms reduced to simple geometrical equivalents in terms of ovals and cylinders. But in both these pictures the abstract elements are still pretty well disguised by the apparent semiphotographic character of the images. The average

observer experiences a certain emotional reaction from looking at "Whistler's Mother" and quite naturally attributes his reaction to his liking for the subject, without giving a thought to the arrangement of quiet shapes and quiet colors that are doing so much to produce his reaction. He has a different response to the Renoir and attributes it to the difference in subject—a young, vital, blossoming woman instead of a gentle, resigned old lady. Naturally the reaction to the subject plays a large part, but actually the freshness of Renoir's color and the fine vigorous solidity of the forms he creates (not imitates) are doing the major part of the job.

The psychological importance of form, color, and arrangement *as* form, color, and arrangement, quite aside from what they happen to be describing, is apparent in both pictures if we imagine what "Whistler's Mother" would look like in bright pinks, blues, and yellows, with rich, sparkling brushwork like Renoir's, instead of Whistler's muted colors and quiet paint surface. Renoir's portrait of his wife would be a curious picture indeed if the fresh and vital image were painted in dull grays and blacks or recreated in the quiet subdued silhouettes of Whistler's portrait of the old lady.

Still, for the average observer awareness of their abstract elements is not necessary for a partial understanding of these two pictures. Both of them can be appreciated from a semiphotographic point of view, even if not fully appreciated. But by the time we reach a picture like Marin's *Singer Building* (Plate 29, Portfolio 3) we find abstract elements dominating realistic ones. In the lower half Marin expressed the noise, the movement, the excitement and confusion of the city by a composition of slashing angles, lines, and colors that only half resembled the actual objects involved. In this painting we must recognize and accept abstraction to enjoy the picture at all. The artist seems to say that if a subject can be expressed through angles, lines, shapes, colors, arrangement, and other abstract elements, there is no reason why he has to depend any longer on even semiphotographic reality. Is there then any reason to give us any recognizable images at all? Perhaps abstract elements alone can tell the story. To carry the argument to its logical conclusion, why is it necessary even to have a subject? Why not just have forms, colors, and arrangement by themselves, for their own sake? Marin never went quite this far, but many contemporary painters do.

Now let us say immediately that though this argument sounds logical, it does not necessarily hold true when applied at its extreme limit. It is quite possible that the modern abstract artist is defeating himself when he insists that recognizable images are of no importance in painting and should be left to the camera or (he might say) to those artists without enough creative imagination to get away from painting like a kind of camera. This is the basic dispute of "modern art." The object of this portfolio is not to settle the argument, nor even to take sides. We will examine some modern abstractions, and we will also compare some of them with paintings by old masters or traditional painters who at first glance appear to be working almost photographically. We will begin by comparing two paintings of artists at work in their studios, one by the great seventeenth-century master Vermeer (*The Artist in His Studio*, Plate 37) and one by the leader of modern art, Pablo Picasso (*The Studio*, Plate

38). It would be a good idea to compare the two illustrations, side by side, as you read.

Abstract Values in Realistic Painting

In Vermeer's painting we look into the cube-like space of an artist's studio. This space is defined for us on all six sides. The back wall faces us directly. The front wall is expressed by the heavy curtain drawn aside to let us look within the space as if it were a stage. Without having to think about it or figure it out, we sense the windowed wall to our left by the flow of light onto the model and across the space of the room. The wall to our right is also defined by inference. The chandelier, which would be near the center of the ceiling, helps us locate it, as does the position of the large decorative map on the rear wall and the chair lined up with its edge. The floor and ceiling we actually see.

Within this cube of space Vermeer arranges his figures and objects with exquisite care. We see the painter's back as he faces the canvas on his easel. He is using a mahlstick, a stick used by painters to steady the hand while working on passages of fine detail. Without being able to see his other hand we know that it holds his palette. He is glancing at the model, who is posed as an allegorical figure crowned with leaves and bearing a trumpet and a book (*Figure 1*). We see her across a table that holds, among other things, a cloth hanging off the edge nearest us.

The forms in this Vermeer are not to be regarded as flat silhouettes, as it is possible to regard those in "Whistler's Mother." They must be seen as solid volumes in three-dimensional space—and when a picture like this one is studied and reflected upon, the shape of the voids between these various solid objects can become as interesting as the objects themselves. This painting is a spatial composition.

The little cube-shaped world is wonderfully

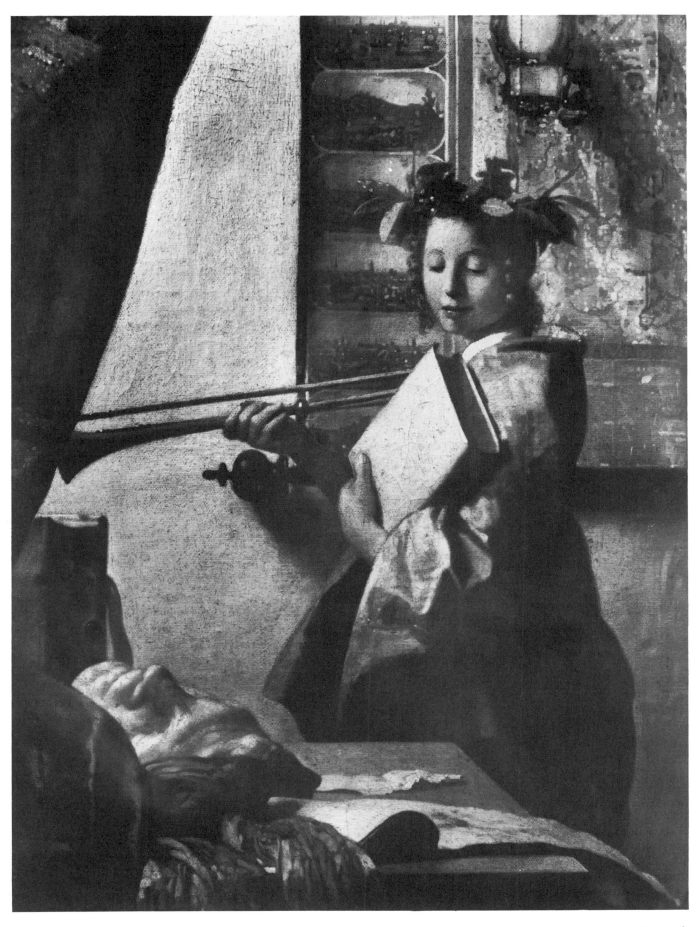

Figure 1

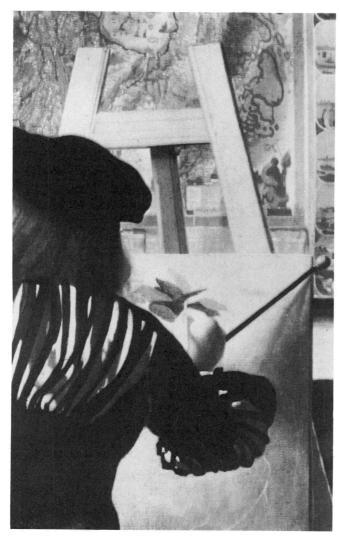

Figure 2

If you can imagine the model looking out the window and the painter turned to regard us, thus completely divorcing the painter and the model and bringing the painter, so to speak, outside the room to where we stand, on this side of the heavy curtain, you will see that the whole structure falls to pieces.

Other changes would be less disastrous, but any change would mar the picture's balance. Would you want to push the artist and the easel farther back into the picture space? Or move them nearer to us, so that they become larger in perspective, leaving more depth between the artist and the model? Would you rather the objects on the table were tidied up, or removed, or added to? Would you like to see the curtain hanging in straight folds, rather than bunched as it is? Would you like to eliminate the series of beams, terminating the picture at its upper part with their succession of horizontal lines, and substitute a flat ceiling?

None of these changes except the elimination of the ceiling beams would make the individual objects any the less interesting. The picture would still be an assemblage of magnificently rendered textures bathed in light. We could still sense the brassiness of the chandelier, the nap of the curtain, the silkiness of the model's robe, the smooth, cool surface of the floor. But the perfection of the picture is not the sum of its wonderful details any more than the beauty of a musical composition is the sum of its individual chords. The perfection of the picture lies in the harmonious union of these details as arranged in space, just as the beauty of music may be in the harmony of the chords arranged in time.

From Realism to Abstraction

Our second picture, Picasso's *The Studio*, is such a close parallel to the Vermeer that it might almost have been painted to demonstrate how the Vermeer could be translated into abstract terms. To understand Picasso, however, we have to begin by accepting his complete

self-contained. There is no feeling that the various objects are rigidly placed, but their relationship in space is so perfect that if we try to shift any one of them the serene balance of the picture is disturbed. Would you, for instance, want the model to turn her head so that, in profile, she looks out of the window? This would be a small change, but it would disrupt the picture. It would make us too conscious of the window wall. We would be tempted to follow the model's gaze into the imagined world outdoors, instead of remaining happily within the defined space of the studio. It would also tend to divide the picture down the middle, since the psychological connection between the painter and the model would be weakened. This connection is like a unifying structural element in the composition.

8

rejection of photographic imitation. This rejection is perfectly obvious in the picture, but it is not easy for most people to accept.

Your first question may be why Picasso chooses to work in a way so radically different and so puzzling, when perfection like the Vermeer can be achieved through an approach almost photographic in individual details. We will try to answer that question, but first—with the illustrations side by side—let us see the similarities between the two pictures. Actually, the similarities are as great as the differences. The painter stands to the left in the Picasso; he sits at the right in the Vermeer. Picasso constructs the figure of the painter in a few dark lines played against the light field of the canvas he is about to work on. Vermeer constructs the figure of his painter as a dark silhouette, also played in part against the creamy field of his canvas, upon which he has just begun to work (*Figure 2*). Both painters hold their brushes in a moment's pause. The "brush" in the Picasso is the short diagonal line terminating the "arm" that projects horizontally toward the right. Whereas Vermeer's artist has just stayed his hand to glance at the model, Picasso suggests by the extended line that his artist is sighting along his brush—a common device—to measure the proportions of the object he is painting.

The painter's "head" is a long gray oval form upon which is imposed an irregular white shape bearing three eyes arranged in a vertical row (*Figure 3*). Whether or not it was the artist's intention, we may hazard the guess that the painter is given this extra eye as a kind of symbol of the particularly acute, analytical vision developed by an artist in comparison with the average person, who sees more casually.

The painters in both pictures hold palettes, although we see neither of them. In the Vermeer we sense the palette. In the Picasso it is symbolized by its thumb hole, a small circle just to the left of the painter's shoulder.

Vermeer's painter is working from a posed

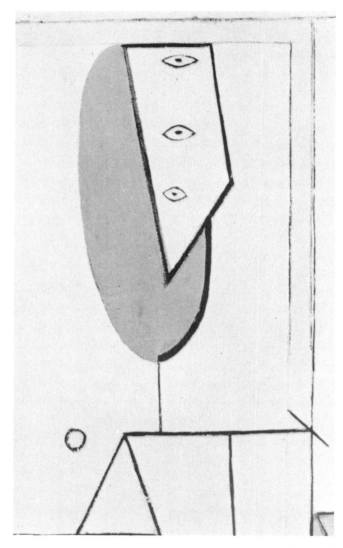

Figure 3

model; Picasso's from a still-life setup composed of a plaster bust and a bowl of fruit on a table. A red cloth hangs from the side toward us, as in the Vermeer. The irregular white quadrangle is the base of the plaster bust. Within the white oval that suggests its general mass a six-sided shape defined by a black line bears two eyes and a mouth, or perhaps two normal eyes and a "blind" one suggesting the smooth blind eye of a plaster cast, arranged in the same way as the three eyes of the painter. The fruit bowl is reduced to two triangles, the fruit represented by a single green circle in the upper one. All four legs of the table and the round feet are visible, although they are placed arbitrarily, without regard to perspective. The red cloth, with its main lines accentuated by a wide hem, "hangs"

9

in stiff angular shapes that are flat patterns.

Flanking Picasso's painter on the side of the picture opposite him there is also a window, or glassed door, and on the back wall hang a framed picture and a dark mirror, rectangles only slightly more regular than the one of the decorative map hanging on the corresponding wall in the Vermeer.

These details add up to a close similarity between the pictures, even granting some leeway to their interpretation in the Picasso. The final similarity, and a most important one, is that each of the compositions is tied together by an invisible element—a cord of interest vibrating between the painter and the model. We have already commented on this in the Vermeer, saying that if the model looked out the window or if the painter turned his head to look at us, the beautiful integration of the cube of space would be lost. In the Vermeer this connection between model and painter goes back into the depth of space. In the Picasso it plays across the surface of the picture between the dominating lines and shapes abstracted from the painter and his still life.

Why Abstraction?

But why has Picasso chosen to paint this way, instead of following Vermeer's tradition, one that satisfied painters for so long? Picasso was something of a child prodigy. In his teens he had already mastered the conventional techniques of painting and drawing. Why did he abandon them? He has had to sacrifice a great deal in order to work abstractly. First of all he sacrifices—for most people—the interest inherent in the objects comprising the picture, an interest on which Vermeer capitalizes. Next, he sacrifices the fascination and variety of natural textures. He sacrifices the harmonies of flowing light, the satisfaction of building solid forms out of light and shade.

What has he gained?

He has gained complete freedom to manipulate the forms in his picture. He need not bother with the true proportions of objects or their parts. If for the sake of design or expression he wants to make a head three quarters the size of the body beneath it, he may do so. He may adjust every shape within his picture area quite arbitrarily. If he has sacrificed the advantages of perspective, which would have permitted him to create an illusion, he has also gained freedom from its limitations, which would have forced him to show the table legs, the bust, or any of the other objects according to a rigid system. For perspective is after all only a systematic distortion by which objects are shown larger or smaller and at different angles from their real ones in order to represent their position in a third dimension, and all according to rule. Picasso's distortion is his own, not that of a geometrical system.

But all these sacrifices and gains are only part of a means to an end. What is the argument in favor of the end Picasso has in view?

The abstractionist would argue that the enjoyment of a picture like Picasso's *The Studio* is more intense because it is purer than the enjoyment we take in the Vermeer. We more fully enjoy pure form, pure color, and pure arrangement because we are less diverted by incidental interests. In the Vermeer we are diverted by our interest in the map on the wall, by our curiosity about the details of the model's costume, by our surprise at the novel cut of the painter's blouse, and by all the other items that are curious or interesting in themselves. The traditional painter would argue that the enjoyment of the Vermeer is richer for the very reason that it may be enjoyed simultaneously on the double score of its abstract merits and its associative interests. But such a discussion eventually boils down to the conclusion that a great painting is a great painting, regardless of its means.

Many people have the uncomfortable feeling that modern abstract art is too easy because the painter is not obliged to demonstrate a high degree of craftsmanship. The Vermeer, considered as craftsmanship alone, remains a gem. Technically and in details it is an extremely complicated picture, but in this very complication there is a degree of safety that is denied to the abstract painter. The Picasso is so simplified that any faulty relationship would be more glaring than one in the Vermeer. A second-rate picture along the lines of the Vermeer is still an interesting picture, can even be a good one. A second-rate picture along the lines of the Picasso is simply no good at all.

By examining the structure of the Picasso we can discover, if we have not felt it from the first, that the picture is as tautly constructed as Vermeer's is exquisitely arranged. We cannot read it in depth the way we read the Vermeer (although it is possible to discover some shallow recessions and projections of its flat planes), but we can apply something of the same test of shifting or changing forms and colors. The most obvious element tying the picture together is the repetition of strict verticals and horizontals. Then there are other parallels or near parallels, such as the left edge of the red cloth, which parallels the right line of the main triangle of the figure of the artist, and the top left line of the plaster bust, which parallels the right side of the fruit bowl. The line of the artist's "neck," if continued downward, meets the intersection of two other lines and forms one side of a suggested square. The top of the fruit bowl, continued to the right, would meet the point of balance of the bust on its pedestal. A dozen similar relationships can be discovered; they form a kind of secondary, concealed but important, supporting structure. As in the Vermeer, every element in the Picasso affects every other one. The thumb hole of the palette, to take an example at random, seems just the right size and in just the right spot; if it were made a brilliant color, this change would have to be compensated for by shifting its position or changing its size, or both. This is bringing things down to a fine point, but a picture like *The Studio* depends on fine points. There is no room for accidental

or unconsidered elements. True, it takes time and adjustment to new ideas to see these points in abstract painting, but the effort is worth making if it opens up a new field of enjoyment.

There is no point in saying that the Picasso is better than the Vermeer or that the Vermeer is better than the Picasso. Both are superb achievements. You may prefer one or you may prefer the other, but there is no reason why both cannot be deeply rewarding. To accept one and to reject the other could be an indication that the preferred picture is being enjoyed for superficial reasons. People who like the Picasso because it is fashionable to like modern art are making the same mistake as people who like the Vermeer because it is a sign of "culture" to like an established, foolproof old master. Neither picture can·bring its full reward on such superficial bases. Either picture, enjoyed through full understanding, increases enjoyment and understanding of the other.

Tradition and Revolution

Having compared one realistic masterpiece with an abstract one, stressing their similarities, we will compare another realistic traditional painting with an abstraction to show how violently they may differ. Nearly three hundred years separated Vermeer's painting from the Picasso we have just seen, yet we found in them a fundamental similarity. Only seven years separate Sargent's *The Wyndham Sisters* (Plate 39) from Picasso's *Les Demoiselles d'Avignon* (Plate 40), but they could hardly be more different.

The Wyndham Sisters is a stunning technical display celebrating aristocratic fashions. Sargent was one of the most facile painters who ever lived. These yards and yards of satin, these explosions of flowers, these opulent glints of gold in the shadowy depths of a mansion, these delicately boned faces, and these graceful figures with their languorous hauteur and easy elegance, all are brushed across the surface of the canvas as if effortlessly. Everything is very cool and very expensive and just a little patronizing in its suggestion that all this privileged refinement is on display for us to look at, to marvel at, to admire, to envy, but not to touch. It is as if the ladies, having opened their mansion for charity, have had the further graciousness to incorporate themselves into the decor for the afternoon. Without this little seasoning of condescension the picture would not be the consummate expression of Edwardian fashion that it is.

satisfying. Within that intention it is an unqualified success. It is a picture we may enjoy wholeheartedly for its obvious attractions, as we could not do if it pretended to offer anything more.

It is easy to see why a public habituated to pictures like *The Wyndham Sisters* would be horrified by the sudden appearance of pictures like *Les Demoiselles d'Avignon*. By the standards of fashionable painting in 1907 *Les Demoiselles* is a perfectly ghastly picture.

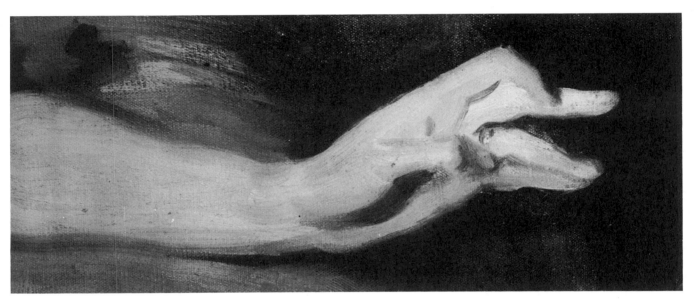

Figure 4

The Wyndham Sisters is an extremely attractive picture, but it is virtually without abstract interest. The arrangement is casual—skillful enough, but not rewarding in itself. The brushwork is breathtaking (*Figure 4*), in the same sense that it is breathtaking to see a magician pull a rabbit out of a hat. But the painting's real interest, its real reason for being, lies in its stylish reproduction of its stylish subjects. There is no point in hunting for hidden depths, no point in exploring beneath immediate appearances. The merit of the picture is not in its profundity but in its finality: it is the fashionable portrait to end all fashionable portraits (*Figure 5*). It is a reflection rather than an interpretation of an attitude toward life. It is intended to be visually pleasing rather than emotionally stimulating or intellectually

The women are ugly (*Figure 6*), there is no dazzling technical display, the drawing is so bizarre that you can't even tell where some of the forms begin and end. Above all, the whole thing looks inept, if not perhaps insane. The most generous thing one of the Wyndham sisters might have found to say about the picture is that it must be a joke. Or if the artist is serious, the poor fellow must have lost his reason. If, however, Picasso is insane he certainly holds the all-time record for remaining conspicuously at large. And while a few people will still claim that modern art is an enormous hoax or a sensationalized bid for attention, *Les Demoiselles d'Avignon* was for Picasso a self-imposed labor of creative analysis and was not even exhibited until thirty years after it was completed.

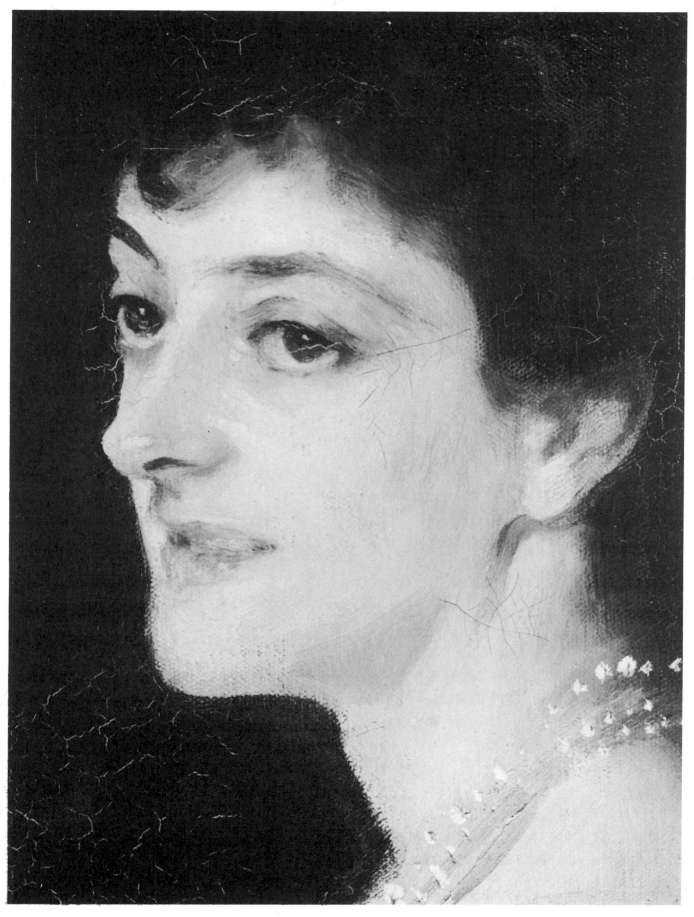

Figure 5

We have already said that while Picasso was still in his teens he had mastered the craft of drawing and painting as understood by Sargent's public; in his twenties he had already rejected it. *Les Demoiselles d'Avignon*—a huge picture—is a prodigious effort to discover new means of expression, not for the sake of their newness but for the sake of increasing the scope and intensity of the art of painting.

We need not pretend that *Les Demoiselles* is a completely successful painting. It is a masterpiece in the sense of being a landmark everyone interested in painting should know, rather than a picture to be enjoyed solely in its own right. It could hardly be a completely successful picture, for it was painted at the beginning of a revolution so great that it is still going on today. If we compare it with *The Studio*, painted nearly thirty years later, we can sense that it lacks the assurance, the final satisfying sense of completeness of the latter work. But it is still a painting of tremendous force and vigor. If it were not, it could not impress, irritate, and hold people as it does. What we must remember is that it is first of all an intellectual exercise in abstraction, an effort to evolve and apply new theories that were to crystallize into cubism, a new way of analyzing forms in painting (*Figure 7*). We will return to *Les Demoiselles d'Avignon* in a later portfolio when it is time to explain some of these theories.

The chief fault of *Les Demoiselles*, one that keeps it from being a satisfying picture in its own right, is exactly the fault that the average layman is first likely to find with it: we are never able to break away from the fact that these *demoiselles* are, after all, five exceptionally unlovely female figures. No matter how hard we try to argue ourselves into seeing them as satisfactory abstractions, they remain thoroughly unsatisfactory women. They have not been "abstracted" to the point where we can dissociate them from our perfectly legitimate and inevitable ideas of what a human figure should be. Abstraction has merely deformed them, and the deformations are not of a

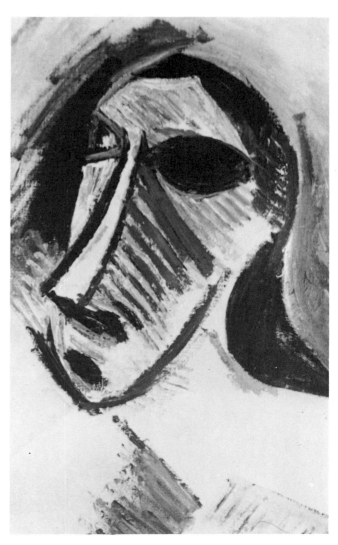

Figure 6

kind to clarify or intensify our reaction, as in the case of expressionism. The young experimenter has not been able to resolve the conflict between reality and abstraction, as we saw the mature man do in *The Studio*, where the objects retain a very real importance yet have fully realized abstract character.

Nonobjective Painting

Some painters believe that there is such a fundamental contradiction between painting abstractly from real objects (no matter how abstracted) that if a painting is going to be abstract at all it should be totally so, with no connection whatsoever with the world of visible reality. Such painting is frequently called *nonfigurative* or *nonobjective* to distinguish it

14

from the kind of abstraction that has even a tenuous connection with the world we see. Mondrian's *Rhythm of Straight Lines* (Plate 41) is a nonfigurative painting that seems so puzzling and pointless to the average person that we will try to explain it by asking a series of questions similar to the ones most frequently asked by gallerygoers faced by it, answering them in quotations or paraphrases from Mondrian's own written explanations of his theories:

Question: Why do you call this a painting when it is only some black lines and a few rectangles of color?

Answer: All painting—the painting of the past as well as of the present—is made up of lines and color.

Q: Yes, I know, but in the pictures I like the line and color are used to describe forms of things I recognize and like.

A: But all those things you recognize and like actually exist in nature as solid objects. The painter has to reduce them to the flat plane surface of his canvas. If we forget about natural appearances we can free line and color on this plane surface.

Q: A lot of painters paint rather flatly. Whistler's *Arrangement in Gray and Black* is composed of essentially flat shapes and Picasso's *The Studio* looks completely flat to

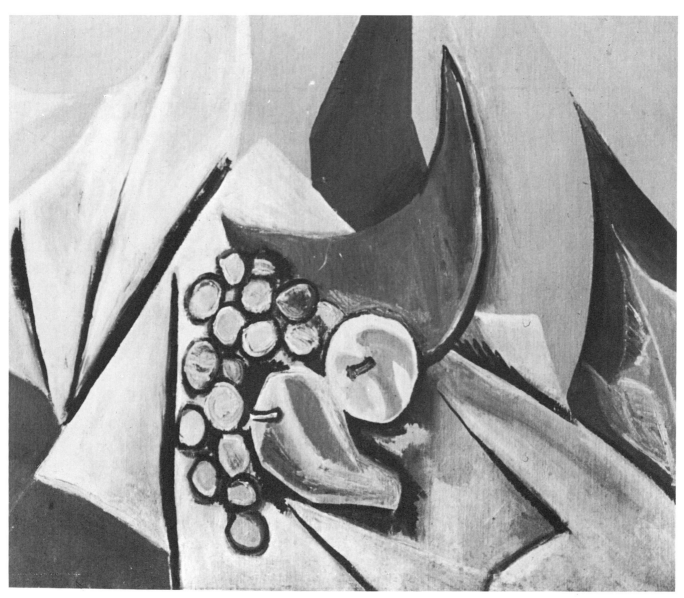

Figure 7

15

me. But those pictures mean something. Yours doesn't.

A: Those were steps in the right direction. But art should be a *universal* expression. Whistler's *Arrangement* isn't universal because you can identify the forms as individual objects and the old lady as an individual old lady. Picasso's forms are more universal because they are more abstract. But mine are completely universal because I have used only a single universal form: the rectangular area in varying dimensions.

Q: That is a logical argument, but the forms are still meaningless to me.

A: Not meaningless. Neutral. All associative values are annihilated, so line and color are completely freed.

Q: But it seems so cold, so mechanical.

A: I mean it to. I think that for the modern mentality a work of art should have the appearance of a machine or a technical product.

Q: If you feel that way, I don't see why you wouldn't get more satisfaction out of being a mechanic, rather than an artist.

A: I am not a mechanic. I am a living machine, capable of realizing in a pure manner the essence of art.

Whether or not you find it possible to concur with Mondrian's theories, it is true that his art is close to an ultimate statement of the contemporary painter's tendency to attach less and less importance to subject matter and more and more to theory. We refer once more to Whistler's effort to deny the subject and emphasize theory in *Arrangement in Gray and Black* by giving it the title he did. Mondrian also says that his art is not opposed to nature but quite the reverse, since he seeks a "dynamic equilibrium," which he calls the first law of nature.

We can even discover that his nonfigurative painting developed from his early, fairly realistic works. The *Landscape with Farmhouse* (Plate 42) was painted about 1906. The house, and particularly its reflection in the canal, already gives a hint of his effort to find order

by reducing forms to rigid, strongly defined rectangles of color (*Figure 8*). The bare tree branches are beginning to resolve themselves into a tight pattern more interesting as pure pattern than as branches silhouetted against the sky (*Figure 9*). This means that his treatment is already half abstract; he is well on his way to the much more abstract study *Horizontal Tree* (Plate 43), done five years later. We can still find the general form of a tree in this abstraction, but it is the idea of tree, not the look of tree, that he is analyzing here. Certainly the lines as abstracted and combined by Mondrian express a rhythmic growth fundamental to the idea of a tree. The point in

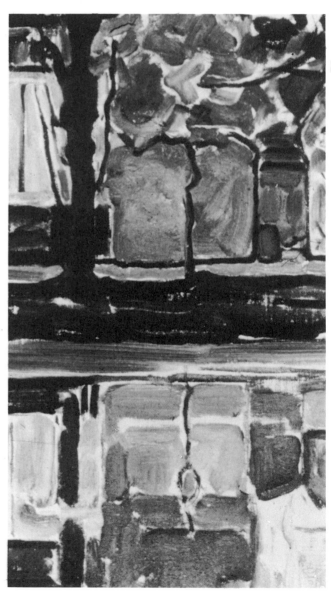

Figure 8

16

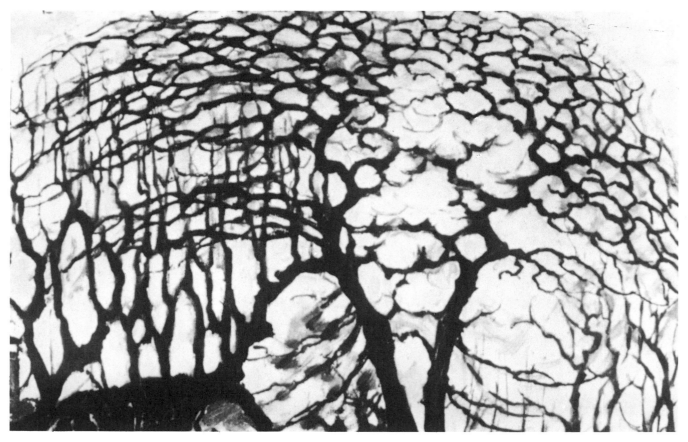

Figure 9

comparing this abstract tree with his more realistic early one is to show that even while Mondrian was still working from nature he was seeking to express nature's "dynamic equilibrium." He did this by reducing the visual world to a kind of geometry—as countless painters have done in different ways. We saw Renoir doing it in his own way in the portrait of his wife (Plate 3, Portfolio 1). Mondrian developed his nonfigurative art along the same approach. We can easily trace this progressive abstraction by comparing a half-tone reproduction (*Figure 12*) of the *Horizontal Tree* of 1911 with three other studies of trees: *Blue Tree* (*Figure 10*), painted in 1909; *Gray Tree* (*Figure 11*), painted in 1910; and *Apple Tree in Bloom* (*Figure 13*), painted in 1912. When we follow through the idea in this way Mondrian's abstractions are not puzzling at all—whether or not they are satisfying. The paradox in Mondrian's art is that his complicated theories have produced paintings of an apparently elementary simplicity.

His logic has produced, for the layman, an art without content or structure. His *Plus and Minus* (*Figure 14*) may look like child's play or doodling—but it is actually the result of an analytical process that began with the artist's response to the look of nature—in this case, to the pattern of tree branches.

Abstraction and Emotional Expression

In our first portfolio we contrasted a Cézanne (Plate 8) with a Durand landscape (Plate 7), saying that Cézanne sought to show an essential orderliness in nature, while Durand regarded nature as a manifestation of mysterious forces. If we had to put all artists into one of two groups, one group would be made up of those who tend to intellectualize and the other of those who tend to emotionalize their subject matter. This is true in abstraction as well as elsewhere. All the abstract paintings we have

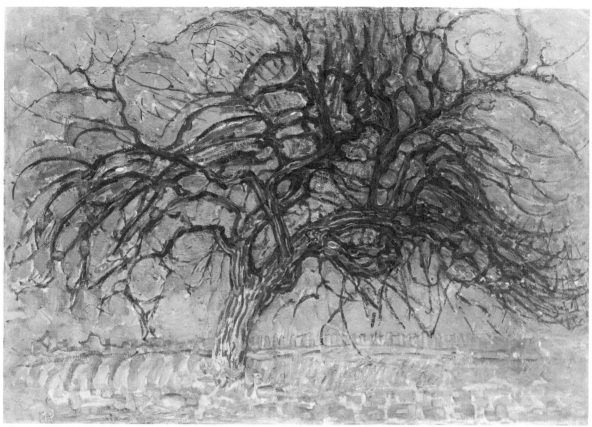

Figure 10

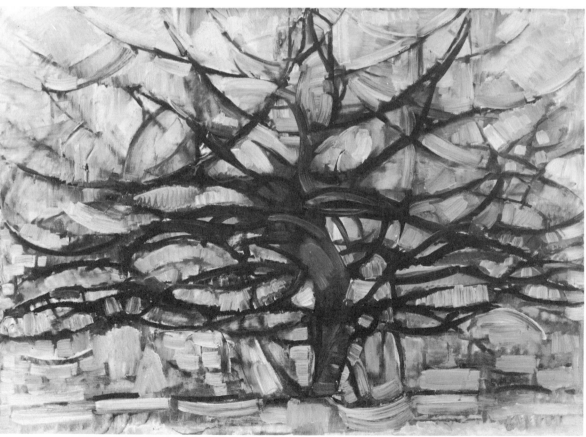

Figure 11

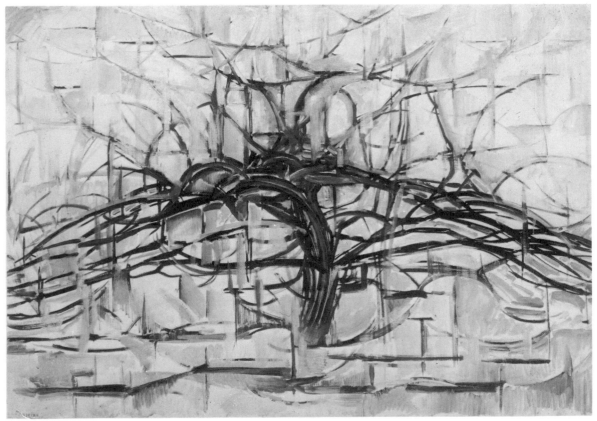

Courtesy Sidney Janis Gallery, New York

Figure 12

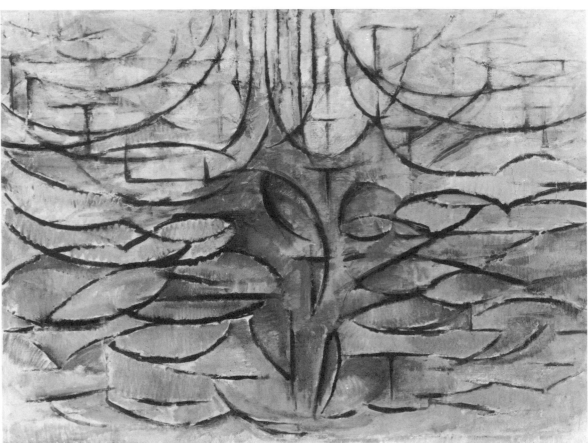

Courtesy Sidney Janis Gallery, New York

Figure 13

19

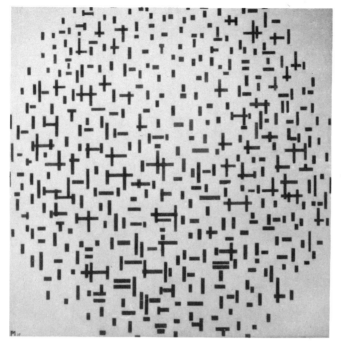

Rijksmuseum Kröller-Müller, Otterlo

Figure 14

seen so far in this portfolio would fall in the first classification, but if we go back again and examine Marin's semiabstract painting of a city (Plate 29, Portfolio 3) we have a clue to our next illustration, Kandinsky's *Black Lines* (Plate 44), which is a piece of emotionalized abstraction—or emotionalized nonobjective painting, if you prefer that term.

A glance shows that this painter is not working with the calculation, the analytical approach apparent in our other examples. The painting appears to be, and is, an improvisation, a kind of free invention. We are not supposed to interpret the lines and areas of color into abstractions of any actual objects. If we tried we might find suggestions of large anemonelike flowers with black stamens, or of sunset clouds, of butterflies or exotic insects, depending on what direction our imagination took. But this would defeat the painter's intention.

Then what is he expressing? Why doesn't he at least give us a clue by a more suggestive title? If he is trying to express a certain mood by using certain shapes and colors, are we expected to play detective to discover what the mood or idea is?

Quite the contrary. The painting is not an emotional anagram. The artist's idea is that a painting should be a creation independent of any outside supporting factors. If it is possible to translate the various combinations of shapes and colors back into real objects or to translate their "meaning" into words, then the painting fails, because it would then have derived its meaning in the first place from ideas or emotions that can be described specifically in something other than pure form and pure color.

Of course, while the painter is at work his choice of shapes and color and the combinations he puts them into is presumably determined by whatever complex of emotions and thoughts is stimulating him to paint in that particular way at the moment. But it is a mistake to try to pin the meaning down. We all know that red suggests excitement, that blue suggests quiet or melancholy, that a jagged line suggests action, while a curved one may suggest relaxation, and a twisted one turbulence, and so on, through a long list of ideas associated with color, shape, and line. But we cannot take the different shapes in *Black Lines* and decide what each one "feels" like, list them, and then say that the painting is a mood comprised of those factors. The painting is what it is. It is "about" itself. What you get from it depends on your sensitivity to its shapes and colors.

But why can't just anybody sit down with a few pots of paints and improvise an abstraction like this one? To a limited extent anybody can, with Kandinsky at hand to be imitated. But the person who tried to do so would be in the position of a person who sets about to prepare an elaborate dinner without ever before having so much as scrambled an egg. We can supply him with all the ingredients and recipes in the most complete detail, but the dinner is going to be inedible. Kandinsky's "recipes" are the accumulated knowledge and experience that every good painter works from, whether he is modern, conservative, abstract, or whatever. For all its spontaneity, *Black Lines* is an application of this knowledge and experience. The painting is an improvisation, but it is improvised from resources that have become second nature to the painter.

Abstraction and New Ways of Seeing

One advantage of becoming acquainted with abstract painting and trying to understand its theories, whether we ever get to the point of fully enjoying it or not, is that nonabstract painting may mean more to us as a result.

Turner's *The Burning of the Houses of Parliament* (Plate 45) is likely to mean more to us after we have tried to understand Kandinsky than it did before. This might have surprised both Turner and Kandinsky, but the advantage is ours.

Turner's picture shows the great conflagration that destroyed the Houses of Parliament in London in 1834. We see the spectacle across the Thames. Crowds of spectators are eerily suggested, but the real play of interest is between the spectacular area at the left, its flames, smoke, air, and water, and the quieter, stabler form of the bridge on the right. As an illustration of an event the painting is dramatic

Figure 15

21

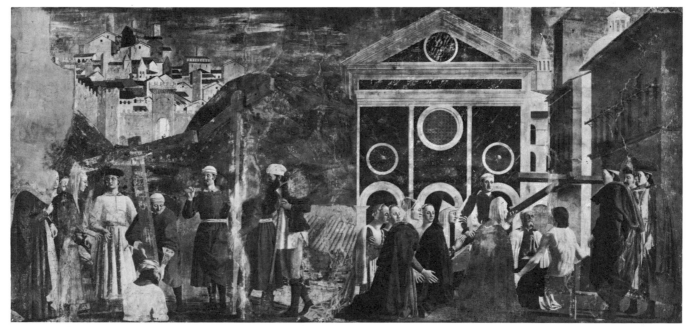

Photo by Anderson

Figure 16

in the extreme. Everyone is fascinated by a good fire, and this one has the additional interest of involving an important and familiar place. We may be interested first by the fire and smoke and steam because they are fire and smoke and steam and in the bridge because it is dramatically crowded—impromptu bleachers for the gigantic spectacle. But if we see the picture more than a few times, its enduring interest will grow in other directions. Our first acquaintance with it—with any subject picture—is on the most obvious level. *The Burning of the Houses of Parliament* will always be a picture of a good fire, but it is a picture of a good fire because Turner has abstracted from the holocaust a magnificent passage of pure painting (*Figure 15*) where incandescent yellows and oranges, purplish blacks, and delicate grays not only say fire, water, smoke, air, and stone, but can give pleasure in themselves as yellows, oranges, blues, and grays, in forms that range from solid, sharply defined ones to spreading, dissolving ones. We could never find between the Kandinsky and the Turner a connection as close as the one between the Vermeer and Picasso's *The Studio*, but the enjoyment of either the Turner or the Kandinsky can in-

crease our enjoyment of the other. It is not necessary that we be conscious of any connection between the pictures, of course. But we may be certain that every picture we see looks a little different and is a little richer for every one we have deeply enjoyed before.

A revolution as extensive as the one that has produced such quantities of abstract art in the past fifty years must also affect the way we see the art of the past. Our understanding of the old masters is not a static thing; from generation to generation new ways of thinking and feeling show us new aspects of a painting or blind us to aspects that were understood and admired not so many years ago.

One old master who has come into his own as a result of our new interest in abstraction is the Italian renaissance painter Piero della Francesca. He has always been regarded as an important painter, but it is only within recent years that his name has appeared on most critics' and painters' lists of the dozen or so greatest painters of all time. We are reproducing a section (Plate 46) of one scene from his great series painted between 1452 and 1466 on the choir walls of the church of San Francesco in the small city of Arezzo. (This scene is shown in full in *Figure 16*.) The whole series tells the Legend of the True Cross. Our illustration shows the Empress Helena directing the excavation of three crosses, that of Christ and those of the two thieves, on the hill of Golgotha outside Jerusalem.

This, then is a storytelling painting. What are the abstract qualities that raise it to the first rank of the world's masterpieces?

First of all, we should be able by now to enjoy the arrangement of forms in the same general way as in the Vermeer. The "stage" this time is extremely shallow, but within its limited depth the figures are arranged as solid, three-dimensional forms, not as flat shapes.

But the spatial relationship of the figures, which accounted for the intimate appeal of the Vermeer, does not, somehow, fully explain the powerful expressive quality of *The Discovery of the True Cross*. The rest of the explanation lies in the created form of the individual figures. Each one has the solidity, the dignity, the quietness of a great natural object or the abstract beauty of a superb architectural work. Some of the figures, with the regular vertical folds of their robes, are as much like fluted columns as human beings (*Figure 17*).

Now, the events pictured here are dramatic, exciting ones, full of action—the digging up of the crosses, the excitement of discovery. Yet the figures show no agitation, no amazement, no movement. They seem hardly to be taking part in these astounding events. Another painter would have twisted them into every attitude of astonishment, would have filled his whole picture with movement and contrast, would have picked us up and carried us along as participants, taking advantage of every theatrical element the story offers.

But Piero della Francesca does not want to illustrate a spontaneous human reaction to spectacular events. He does not regard these miracles as mere exciting anecdotes. He removes his narrative from the plane of worldly experience and invests it with solemnity, grandeur, and reverence. His figures are not

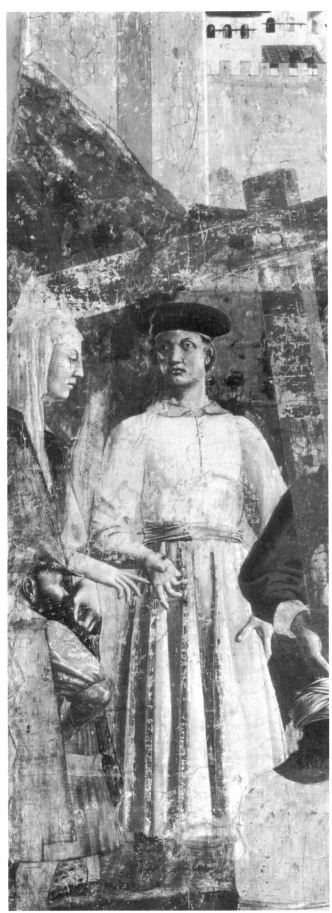

Photo by Anderson

Figure 17

23

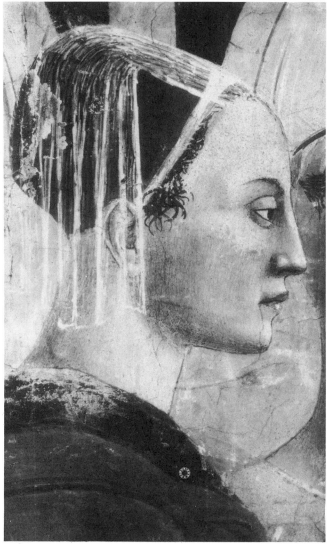

Figure 18

first of all human beings; they are first of all pure form. They are, in a word, abstract. From them we can read the story of the pictured events, but not in human, worldly, or emotional terms. We are not picked up and carried away as participants. If it were possible for us to enter the picture, we would wander around in it unseen, and certainly out of place, among these stately, motionless forms.

This stateliness, this abstract reserve, explains why the art of Piero seemed stiff, cold, and limited not many years ago when people looked first of all for sentiment and emotional drama in religious painting. But we now see in his art an abstract majesty that lifts the events to an appropriately noble level. By comparison, some of the most popular religious

paintings of a generation ago begin to look superficial or even irreverent.

In color as well as in form Piero is subtly unreal. Every color is modified or slightly neutralized. Instead of pure greens he gives us sage and olive; instead of pure reds, rust or brick or plum. His whites, modified toward pearly grays and creams, are as rich as his colors.

A painting like this one, tremendous in size and painted directly on the wall of a church, must lose more of its true quality than other illustrations even in the best color reproduction. The illustration is of necessity so reduced in size that it is possible to hold it in our hands and see all of it at a glance. But the original is so large that as we stand before it our eyes do not see the entire picture so quickly but must travel across it. Sensitivity to the individual forms is increased as they reveal themselves to us gradually. For that reason, the illustration may bring you closer to the original if you cover parts of it and study only a few details at a time or if you move a book or sheet of paper slowly across the illustration from left to right, revealing the figures in sequence. In this way you may become more aware of their variety and even get a somewhat better impression of their size and dignity (*Figure 18*).

Abstract Art and the Future

People frequently ask whether abstract art will last. They also ask whether the extremest forms of abstract art, now that they are a generation old, are more acceptable to very young people than they are to the generation who first saw them.

It is improbable that so large a proportion of the most energetic creative talents of a century can have gone into an art that will disappear. Art flows from the deepest sources of life. Abstract art has persisted in the face of revilement and discouragement for so long that it obviously springs from profound forces within our time. And even if a reaction of sorts should set in against it—and there are indications that this is happening—modern abstract painting will always last, in a historical sense at least, as one of the most stimulating episodes in the history of art. And if abstract painting should finally become nothing more than historical recollections on museum walls, it will live in the modifications it has brought about in less adventurous forms of painting and in the re-evaluations of the art of the past that it has suggested.

It does seem true that the younger a person is the more likely he is to take abstract art in his stride. Youngsters nowadays are less insistent than their parents that a painting look like something else. A time lag between the artist's creation and the public's acceptance of new art forms is characteristic of the past hundred years. We have only to remember that Renoir, a popular idol today, was associated with the early difficult days of impressionism, which was a scandal during his youth and was still thought of as "modern" during a good part of the lifetime of many people who will be reading this discussion.

The lag has been even greater in the case of Cézanne and is not yet entirely taken up. When we look at his *Rocks: Forest of Fontainebleau* (Plate 47) today we can still understand why it was so puzzling to the public who first saw it. They expected all the associative romantic accessories of bosky glades, mossy rocks, sunlit patches—a picture as a kind of substitute for a picnic. Instead of a polished reproduction of a familiar and well-loved woods, Cézanne created a superb abstraction of geometrical forms. Why do we accept it so easily now? Because its revolutionary principles have been pushed so much further by contemporary painters. In being exposed to the latest developments, even if we don't understand them, we are brought to the point where we can enjoy the next to latest. We may still wonder why Cézanne's painting infuriated the public—until we realize how much Picasso's infuriates part of the public today. But

a generation has been born who will look at *The Studio* or *Les Demoiselles d'Avignon* from the perspective the rest of us now have on *Rocks: Forest of Fontainebleau*. They will not be infuriated, and probably their children won't even be puzzled.

Realism, expressionism, abstraction — in these opening portfolios we have tried to isolate them, but a review of the illustrations so far will show that in the majority of cases they fuse, in different proportions, in all painting. The world we see around us, the world of our emotions, and the world of pure intellect are all parts of the same world and they are all part of the world of painting. With this portfolio we reach a dividing line. We have made a partial answer to our original question, "What is a painting?" and are ready to begin a series of portfolios that will bring us closer to the way an artist works—to some principles of pictorial composition and a consideration of techniques and materials.

In the meantime, our final illustration in this first series of portfolios is Gauguin's *Ia Orana Maria* (Plate 48). Painted by a Parisian bohemian self-exiled to the islands of the South Seas, it combines the Christian story of Mary and her Child with the colorful languor of the island people. The picture defies classification into any one of our groups. It is not realistic, but there are realistic elements; it is not expressionist, but it depends somewhat on distortion for its emotional quality—which is the expressionist principle; it is not abstract, except that any carefully studied composition has abstract interest.

Gauguin's treatment of the subject, the Virgin and Child, and the setting, color, and arrangement together create an indefinable mood of poetic mystery. For most people *Ia Orana Maria* is a painting of great immediate appeal. You may or may not want to try to make specific application here of some of the general principles we have been developing. In any case, without further discussion, the picture is left for your enjoyment.

Notes on the Painters

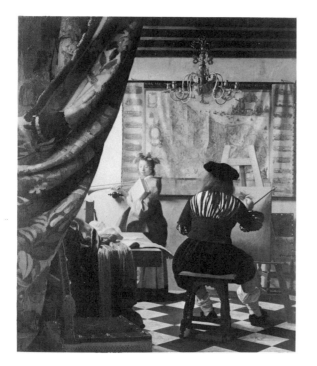

Jan Vermeer, 1632-1675, Dutch

37. THE ARTIST IN HIS STUDIO, 1665-70

Oil on canvas. Height 52⅛". Kunsthistorisches Museum, Vienna

Jan Vermeer of Delft painted, so to speak, in disguise. For the casual observer his compositions of objects, his symphonies of textures, are only subject pictures. This kind of picture makes its appeal to most people through their interest in the subject rather than by the artist's invention. Subject pictures of everyday life were the popular and salable kind of painting in Vermeer's Holland. The practical burghers who were the buyers of paintings were catered to by a group of skillful technicians who have been called the Little Dutchmen. They vied with one another in rendering the shimmer of satin, the softness of the nap of a rug, the polish on wooden furniture, and the stoniness of a floor. They chose immediately recognizable subjects rather than grandiose themes, aimed for literal reality rather than abstraction, and depended more on anecdote than on philosophical expression.

Superficially Vermeer was a member of this group. But his painting is so far above the rank and file of this type that it is impossible to be altogether insensible of his difference from it. His paintings have always been treasured, but it is only recently that his preoccupation with light, space, and texture in abstract terms has received full attention. As with some other old masters— El Greco, for instance—Vermeer's art is revealed to us as much by the theories of contemporary abstraction as by the tradition of his predecessors.

We do not know a great deal about Vermeer's life. There are around forty of his paintings in existence, only a handful in comparison with the number turned out by his contemporaries. The small number is only partially explained by the fact that he died when he was forty-three.

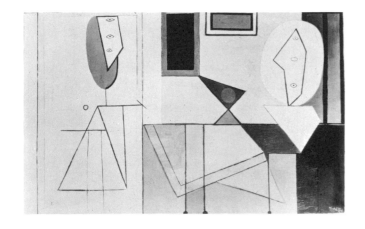

Pablo Picasso, born 1881, Spanish

38. THE STUDIO, 1928

Oil on canvas. Height 59". The Museum of Modern Art, New York, gift of Walter P. Chrysler, Jr.

40. LES DEMOISELLES D'AVIGNON, 1907

Oil on canvas. Height 8'. The Museum of Modern Art, New York, Lillie P. Bliss Bequest

Picasso was born in Spain, but he has spent his creative life in France. No other painter has been so widely published and publicized—a contradictory state of affairs, since no other painter has ever been so incomprehensible and hence so infuriating to the general public. Yet it is impossible to say that Picasso needs no introduction. He does—even those who follow his work from day to day are always being introduced to the latest of its facets.

Of all contemporary painters he is the most productive; it is quite possible that he is the most productive painter of all time. His drawings, paintings, prints, and sculptures run into the tens of thousands, even without such side productions as stage designs and ceramics.

The work of most painters can be classified by the familiar "early," "middle," and "late." This kind of classification is out of the question for

Picasso unless we accept a multitude of subclassifications in each group. He mastered conventional techniques as a youth, took a glance at impressionism, painted for a while like Toulouse-Lautrec. Then Picasso used all these styles as a springboard to a more personal manner, painting emaciated, melancholy figures inspired in equal parts by El Greco and the elongated Romanesque sculpture of certain schools. This, his Blue period, merged with the Rose, when he shifted to this more cheerful color as the dominating one and modified the starveling figures he had been painting into happier, more graceful ones strongly suggesting classical vase paintings and figurines.

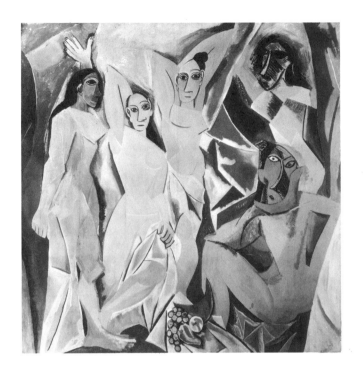

There is a steady continuity to these various early periods. The first decisive break came with his discovery that African sculpture was art as well as anthropology, a discovery made simultaneously by various other restless young painters of the School of Paris. His African period lasted a few months only. It merged into cubism, the major revolution of twentieth-century painting invented by Picasso along with several other artists, the most familiar being Georges Braque (see *Musical Forms*, Plate 15, Portfolio 2), and Juan Gris (1887-1927). Picasso painted *Les Demoiselles d'Avignon* at the point of transition from his African manner to cubism. The faces still suggest African masks, but they and the other forms are also shattered by the analytical procedure of cubism, which tried for simultaneous representation of multiple aspects of an object. But this was only the beginning. Cubism itself has several subdivisions, and Picasso has explored all of them.

Les Demoiselles d'Avignon was painted in 1907. Any effort at an orderly listing of Picasso's ways of working during the subsequent half century is not necessary here, but we can say that they include a sudden shift away from cubism, a reversion to forms as explicit and as tangible as sculpture, and then many variations on the cubist idea, ranging from the humorous to the nightmarish, from happy artifice to great profundity. One of the finest of his intellectual achievements drawing quite directly on some cubist principles is *The Studio*. Also quasi-cubist but lying at the other end of Picasso's expressive range in its intense emotionalism is the great *Guernica*, which may be his masterpiece. (It is considered in Portfolio 6.)

Whether or not you like Picasso you cannot escape him. His influence is so pervasive that many a conservative artist who abominates Picasso paints, all unknowingly, in a way in which he never would have painted if Picasso's art had not been around to flavor his own. The matron who regards Picasso as puzzling usually has a favorite ash tray or print dress with a pattern cribbed by the designer from Picasso.

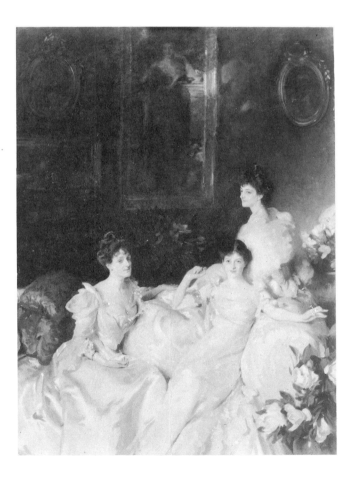

The wearisome accusation is still heard that Picasso is a tongue-in-cheek trickster who is pulling our leg. While this charge is too absurd to answer, it is almost as foolish to expect every Picasso painting to be world-shaking simply because Picasso is a great painter. No man paints that many great pictures, and no man tries to. Because of his range, even more than because of his staggering output, each of Picasso's creations, even more than most painters' work, must be judged on its individual merit. It must be judged by the artist's intention in each particular case—and this is not always easy.

John Singer Sargent, 1856-1925, American

39. THE WYNDHAM SISTERS, 1900

Oil on canvas. Height 9'7". The Metropolitan Museum of Art

Sargent was an American painter trained in France, but his tradition is that of fashionable English portraiture. This tradition places maximum emphasis on a painter's light, brilliant touch and on his ability to achieve an acceptable likeness combined with the most flattering modifications of his sitter's shortcomings as an object of beauty.

From the look of Sargent's portraits each of his sitters was a lady or gentleman of aristocratic distinction. No painter has been more deft than Sargent in the trick of adapting any set of features to the formula of a pre-

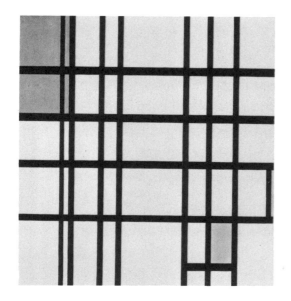

determined type. When you were painted by Sargent you knew in advance that you were going to be magically transformed into a worthy descendant of the beautiful women and handsome men in portraits by Gainsborough, Reynolds, and other painters of the court and the fashionable world of eighteenth-century England.

Unlike these artists, who had only to approximate the sitter's appearance—and sometimes the approximation was not very close, if we are to judge from examples where the same person, painted several times, bears only a family resemblance to himself from picture to picture—Sargent worked in an age when the appearance of the camera forced the painter into greater verisimilitude. Sargent's dazzling concoctions of fact and fiction regarding his sitters are all the more remarkable for that reason.

And yet today his portraits are not very satisfying. We would like to know more about his sitters as people than he has told us. He has not recorded real people; he has left us hundreds of repetitious effigies, variations on an attractive but shallow formula. And Sargent himself is no longer around to charm us with his wit, his urbanity, and all the social graces that were, in effect, part of his fashionable art. His technique seems too glib. He seems to paint so easily that his brush slides over the surface of his subject without penetrating it. His reputation just now is at low ebb, with the first indications appearing of a turn in the tide back to favor.

The condescension with which critics generally treat his art is not altogether justified. The shallow and spectacular quality of the greater part of his work obscures the occasional Sargent painting in which sensitivity outweighs bravado. The final evaluation of his art may be made on the basis of pictures that were thought of as inconsequential during his lifetime.

Sargent achieved the portrait painter's Elysium, where he could choose his sitters and name his prices in foreknowledge that each picture was a success even before he began it, since no picture presented a new problem. Yet he admired the art of Thomas Eakins, who was so unrelenting in his portrayal of his sitters as people that many of his portraits were rejected and some of them were even burned by offended clients. (Compare Plate 39 with Eakins's *Miss Van Buren*, Plate 22 in Portfolio 2.)

Sargent was also one of the most facile of all water-colorists, but here too his technical dexterity has a tendency to eliminate content, as if the picture got finished before Sargent managed to say what he wanted. For Sargent these water colors were an escape from the commissioned portrait into a more personal and creatively more rewarding world.

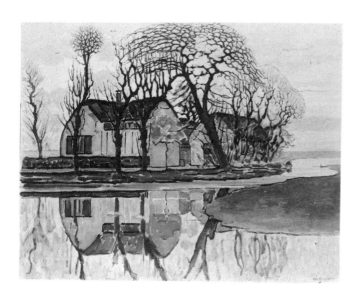

Piet Mondrian, 1872-1944, Dutch

41. RHYTHM OF STRAIGHT LINES, 1936-42

Oil on canvas. Height 28¼". Henry Clifford, Philadelphia

42. LANDSCAPE WITH FARMHOUSE, ABOUT 1906

Oil on canvas. Height 34". Mrs. Isaac Schoenberg, Swarthmore

43. HORIZONTAL TREE, 1911

Oil on canvas. Height 29⅝". Munson-Williams-Proctor Institute, Utica

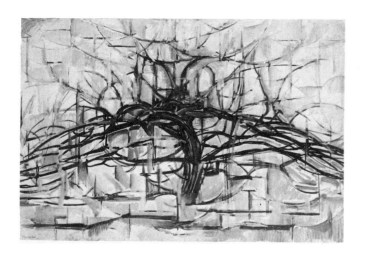

Mondrian was one of a group of painters, architects, and sculptors whose theories (as advanced in their magazine *De Stijl*) formed one of the most potent forces in the crystallization of twentieth-century style. The severity of his rectangular abstractions was shared by the architectural forms favored by *De Stijl*, which today seem less radical than Mondrian's painting to most people because they have become more familiar, often in debased form, in modernistic store fronts.

Actually, it could be argued that these forms are better suited to painting than to architecture, since in the modern world an architecture of pure proportion is limited by practical demands. This would not be true except in the face of the contention that each work in so rarified a style must be purified to the point where slight imperfections are intolerable.

An effort to go even further into abstraction than Mondrian went was made by the suprematists, a Russian group. In 1918 their leader Kasimir Malevich (1878-1935) achieved a white square painted on a white background, entitled *White on White*. It may not be irreverent to suggest that, this having been done, it need not be done again.

Wassily Kandinsky, 1866-1944, Russian

44. BLACK LINES, NO. 189, 1913

Oil on canvas. Height 51¼". The Solomon R. Guggenheim Museum, New York

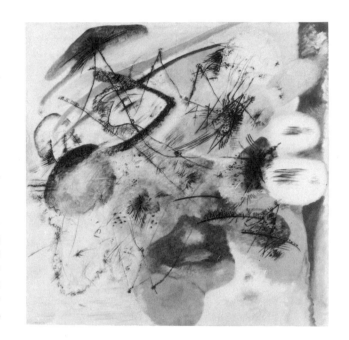

Kandinsky worked with the German expressionists and was one of the original members of the *Blaue Reiter* group formed in 1911 (see Notes on Kirchner, Portfolio 3). We have seen that German expressionism was characterized by free distortion of shapes and arbitrary use of color. Kandinsky follows to its logical conclusion the idea that shape and color, rather than subject, are the expressive factors in painting: he eliminates subject altogether.

Although some of Kandinsky's abstractions have titles, such as *Black Lines*, the title is not chosen to give us a hint about the subject of the painting but only to give it an identification tag. Most of Kandinsky's abstractions are called either composition or improvisation. The compositions are sharply delineated arrangements of precise geometrical forms, but different from Mondrian's in having shapes—and colors—of great variety. The improvisations, on the other hand, are of the type of *Black Lines*—free in execution, with an effect of spontaneity rather than calculation.

Joseph Mallord William Turner, 1775-1851, British

45. THE BURNING OF THE HOUSES OF PARLIAMENT, 1835

Oil on canvas. Height 35". The Philadelphia Museum of Art

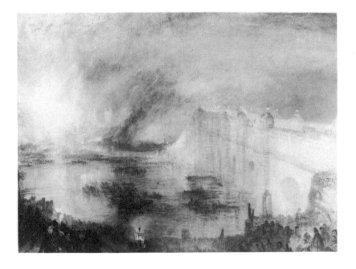

Turner was something of a child prodigy, first exhibiting in the Royal Academy at the age of fifteen. He was tremendously productive and found a ready sale for his work. He began painting conventionally, using a smooth, detailed technique applied to familiar romantic or picturesque subjects. By the time he began to experiment with more abstract approaches, as in *The Burning of the Houses of Parliament*, he was already so well established that the attacks of the critics did him no harm. The collectors continued to buy—when Turner was willing to sell. In his later years he hoarded his own paintings, refusing great sums for them, and on his death he left to the state around two hundred oil paintings and close to twenty thousand drawings.

In Turner's latest paintings the entire picture surface may be nearly as abstract as the left portion of *The Burning of the Houses of Parliament*, where the smoke and flames are not so much a representation of a specific holocaust as an abstract expression of matter in deliquescence. Turner's famous sunsets and storms may turn a whole canvas into areas of swirling, amorphous color suggesting the end of the world, or, more often, its beginning, as forms begin to materialize out of chaos.

Because we have considered Turner in a portfolio devoted to abstraction it may be necessary to point out that he is not part of any abstract tradition on either side of his lifetime. Nor did he think of himself as an abstract painter, nor formulate any theories in that direction. The abstract expressionism we are beginning to see in his work is a matter of hindsight on our part. He did not influence any followers in this direction; rather, he influenced schools of romantic-picturesque landscape (see Durand's *Imaginary Landscape*, Plate 7 in Portfolio 1) that did not have the cosmic suggestion of his own greatest pictures.

Turner was interested in paint and color; he was fascinated by wind, rain, and light. If he approaches abstraction it is because he abandoned the idea of the look of objects in wind, rain, and light in order to seek in paint and color a realization of these forces as ideas.

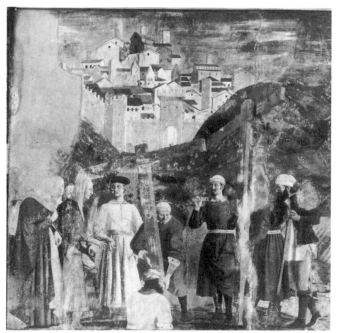

Photo by Anderson

Piero della Francesca, about 1420-1492, Italian

46. THE DISCOVERY OF THE TRUE CROSS, 1452-66

Fresco. Height about 11'. Church of San Francesco, Arezzo

Piero was the author of the first treatise on perspective, a fact that would be meaningless if he had regarded perspective as simply a mathematical formula for the expression of objects in their third dimension. It is that, but for Piero the expression of a third dimension was not an end in itself, nor was it an adjunct to the trick of making things "look real." Piero's art is realistic only if we extend the definition to its extreme limits. In spite of the tangibility of Piero's forms, the logic of their relation to one another, and the accuracy of his perspective, his art is otherworldly. For Piero perspective was a means to the end of creating organized space. His first concern was the disposition of solid volumes in spatial depth. Just what this can mean will become apparent in Portfolio 6, Pictures as Structures, in which two of his other works are discussed.

Piero was a mathematician, as might be deduced from his having codified the laws of perspective. He was also a classical scholar and theoretician on the arts. His own art, correspondingly, is a reserved and intellectual one that cannot be understood in terms of sentiment or surface prettiness. *The Discovery of the True Cross* is from his series of ten huge frescoes in the Church of San Francesco in the small Italian city of Arezzo. These frescoes, which relate the Legend of the True Cross, are among the most impressive achievements in the history of painting. They were commissioned in 1452 and occupied Piero intermittently until 1466.

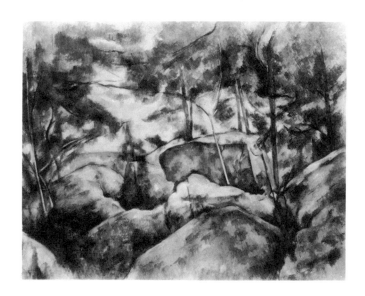

Paul Cézanne, 1839-1906, French

47. ROCKS: FOREST OF FONTAINEBLEAU, 1894-98

Oil on canvas. Height 28⅞". The Metropolitan Museum of Art, H. O. Havemeyer Collection

In discussing *Rocks: Forest of Fontainebleau* and *Mont Sainte-Victoire* (Plate 8, Portfolio 1), we have stressed the classical, abstract quality of Cézanne's art. But Cézanne once said, "I want to make of impressionism something solid and durable, like the art of the museums." He wanted to give to the vibrant, personal, and joyful art of the impressionist painters an air of permanence that he felt it lacked. A good example of the impressionist spirit that he wanted to preserve is found in Manet's *Boating* (Plate 23, Portfolio 2). We feel the charm of the moment, the transient effect of light, the appeal of the commonplace in poetic terms of no very great pretension but very tremendous spontaneous appeal. To combine this spirit with the classical and abstract qualities of more formal, generalized expression was Cézanne's problem. We have dwelt on his formal achievement, but in both the mentioned examples of his work you will probably be able to feel also the element of personal response to nature lying beneath the cooler, more restrained elements of Cézanne's art.

Paul Gauguin, 1848-1903, French

48. IA ORANA MARIA, 1891

Oil on canvas. Height 44¾". The Metropolitan Museum of Art, bequest of Samuel A. Lewisohn, 1951

Gauguin and his friend Vincent van Gogh (see Notes on the Painters, Portfolio 3) have furnished a gold mine of material for writers of popular biographies, plays, films, and fiction. Their lives were bizarre and dramatic, and their paintings supply a ready source of illustration and reference. The result is that alongside a few serious and conscientious biographies we have a quantity of careless and sensational works. Most of these so-called biographies are, more truly, presumptuous works of fiction.

Gauguin abandoned a prosperous business career for the precarious life of a painter. In terms of the average man's idea of a good life this decision was expensive. It cost him his wife and family, his fortune, and the respect of his circle of friends. But there is not much indication that Gauguin suffered a great deal from these sacrifices, although his family and some others probably did. Apparently he felt more than repaid by the violently bohemian life he led from that time on. He painted in Paris, in Brittany, and in the south of France, much of this time with Van Gogh, developing his now familiar but then outlandish style, drawing heavily upon the forms of primitive or ancient art. But it was not until he went to the South Seas, where, except for occasional spectacular forays back to Paris, he spent the rest of his life, that he became the artist whose work is familiar to most of us.

It is important in understanding the art of Gauguin to remember that he did not "go native." He lived with the natives, and he seemed to live as they did. He became absorbed in their legends and superstitions. But Gauguin was always a sophisticate. Like all bohemians he lived outside the life that surrounded him. His first instincts were always self-indulgent. The typical bohemian is a parasite upon the civilization from which he draws sustenance, but of course this parasitism is justified when it feeds a creative talent. This seems to have been Gauguin's attitude, and he never hesitated to sacrifice anyone else's well-being to it.

In the case of Van Gogh we have an obvious answer to the question of why a man chooses to paint and continues to paint in the face of every discouragement. It was for Van Gogh, that unhappy man, an emotional release of an intensely personal nature. In Gauguin's case analysts might find the answer tied up with some kind of exhibitionism necessary to him. W. Somerset Maugham examines his personality in a novel, *The Moon and Sixpence*, that is a truer story of Gauguin's life than many so-called biographies, though Maugham changes names, nationalities, and factual circumstance at will. The story examines motivations without sticking to historical accuracy, whereas the sensational biography may stick to historical accuracy but disfigures it with any distorting overlay promising to increase sales.

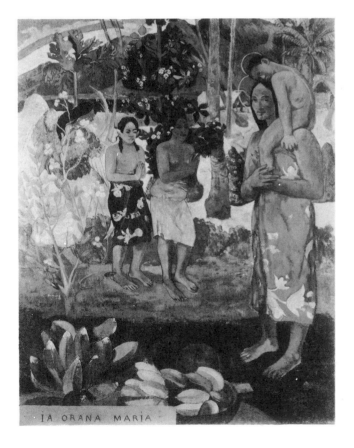

Historically, Gauguin belongs to the postimpressionists, a label covering also Cézanne, Van Gogh, and Seurat, whose work appears in a later portfolio of this seminar. The common denominator of this mixed group is dissatisfaction with impressionism and a desire to seek a way forward from it. Gauguin found his way after imitating Cézanne, infringing briefly upon the style his friend Van Gogh was developing, and trying without much success to subject himself to the rigidly demanding manner of Seurat. He found himself at last in the flat, decorative style of *Ia Orana Maria*, combining elements from ancient Egyptian painting, Japanese art, the art of the Middle Ages, the art of primitive peoples.

Like the other postimpressionists Gauguin is a link between nineteenth-century painting, with its direct reference to the everyday world, and twentieth-century painting, with its abstract emphasis. Much of his work is not much more than ornamental, in a way a painted screen is ornamental. But occasionally he is unexpectedly gentle, even lyrical, as in *Ia Orana Maria*, and often he shows us a glimpse of the dark and ominous world of superstition that lies behind the colorful illusion of happy innocence in primitive life.